Sharon —
I hope you enj

Love
Kathy

SILENT VOICES

Stories Of Survival From The The Great Depression

Interviewed, compiled and written by
Kathleen Shelton

Published by
Kisco Publications
P.O. Box 405
Palermo Ca 95968

SILENT VOICES
Stories Of Survival From The Great Depression

This is a collection of personal stories, interviewed, collected, and written by Kathleen Shelton. Upon publication all stories, poems, ect. become the property of Kathleen Shelton and no payment shall be given for their use.

Library of Congress Catalog Card Number 00 135550

ISBN # 1-893566-10-2

Printed and published in the United States of America by

Kisco Publications
P.O. Box 405
Palermo California 95968

This anthology contains personal stories of ordinary people who lived through and did their best to survive America's most devastating decade since the Civil War.

The Great Depression 1929 - 1939

They survived.

Could we survive?

Does history repeat itself?

I dedicate this book to my parents, their friends, & my friends who's story contributions made this anthology possible.
I regret its lateness but an obstacle beyond my control delayed the publication date.
I apologize for this. I also apologize to the families of some of the contributors, My mother included, who's voices have become silent before their stories could be told. Though their voices may be silent, may their stories live forever.

TABLE OF CONTENTS

SILENT VOICES

Tell me about the drought of long ago.
Tell me of the dust bowl years,
I want to know.
Tell me how you survived.
Tell me how you stayed alive.
Your voice is weakening,
I can hardly hear.
Soon your words will be lost,
and will we care?
Oh, what a terrible cost.
Listen people to your past,
these memories can no longer wait.
For soon these voices will be silent,
and then,
it will be too late.

DEPRESSION DATES

Jessica

I began dating during the depression and was married by the time it ended.

As a teenager I knew our country was in serious trouble. There wasn't enough jobs or money and people were homeless and hungry. But in our little Northern California town we weren't as bad off as other areas.

My father lost his job but my mother taught school in our small one room schoolhouse. So we always had money for food and clothing as did most of the people in our community.

There was no extra money, even if you worked, so our friends and neighbors formed their own entertainment, which was where my dating experiences took place.

Every Saturday afternoon, weather permitting, we gathered at someones house. Usually ours as we had the best yard for the event.

In the afternoons, the adults played cards, checkers, horse shoes, and talked about the economy. Baseball was another favorite game for everyone. But I think the most popular game was the boy's marble shoot. Everyone watched and rooted for their favorite shooter. I watched 10 and 12 year old boys put as much energy in those marble games as my grandson does playing his expensive computer game. There was always a lot of shouting and even a few pennies were lost and won on bets.

The teenagers, if not involved in a game, talked, flirted, held hands and went for walks. If the weather was warm enough we would splash each other in the stream that ran through the back of our property.

At supper time the food was laid out. Every family brought a dish or two so there was always enough food for the biggest appetites.

After eating and while the ice cream was being made, those that brought insterments were busy warming them up for the biggest attraction of the day, dancing.

We danced, laughed, joked and ate ice cream until we were exhausted.

No, we didn't have much money back then but we didn't need money to have fun. Those are some of my fondest memories, especially the summer of 1936 when my husband proposed during a break in the dancing.

What can I say, to me, the depression years were wonderful years.

THE STORM

Mary Elizabeth

I stood in the wind like I was in a trance watching the blackness moving towards me.

It seemed to be rolling..., rollong down from heaven and slowly devouring everything in its path like a huge black monster.

I grasped the porch rail for support as total darkness sent me down into its abyss.

Suddenly strong arms jerked me through an opening to safty. My father slammed the front door, its loud crash brought me back to reality. He held me as I cried and I didn't know why.

My mother said the dust storm had hypontized me.

From my diary April 16, 1934

RIDING THE RAILS

No Name

My family was always poor. I spent the first eleven years of my life in the Appalachia Mountains of West Virginia. My dad was a moonshiner (made illegal whiskey) and when a feud broke out between my family and another moonshinner family over a still we fled the area fearing for our safty or even, our lives. My Uncle and his son had mysteriously disappeared and my father feared some of us would be next.

It was 1934. My dad was uneducated and illiterate and was unable to find work of any kind. There was no money nor no jobs to be had anywhere.

Then someone told my dad about California and about the money people were getting for picking fruit. My dad liked that idea but with no money or transportation getting there posed a problem. Our only hope, he told us was to ride the rails with other hobo families. That trip was like desending into hell.

The trip took about two weeks. Besides my parents, there was me, and my brothers, ages 9, 7, and 3. Eating was our main concern. We had no money, so in the larger towns,my dad would take me and my brothers into the downtown business district and make us beg for money so we could buy food. I know we were a pitiful sight being ungroomed and dirty. I was so embarrassed, but when your stomach is rumbling, you'll do just about anything to get something inside it.

At nights we huddled together in the corner of the box cars trying to sleep. Our dad was always watchful for the railroad bulls. Railroad bulls were big mean men hired by the railroads to keep people like us off the trains.

Our first run in with a bull happened on our third day out. We were climbing into a box car when this huge man came charging at us swinging an iron pipe.

I remember my dad yelling at us to run, we did. It took us the rest of the day to find eachother. My dad had been hit in the shoulder by the bull's pipe but the rest of us were safe.

That night we slept under a bridge with another homeless family. It wasn't comforting knowing there were other families in the same condition we were in.

I can only imagine what we must have looked like when we finally arrived in Bakersfield. We were still wearing the same clothes we'd left West Virginia in. My mom said there was no since in cleaning up as we'd only be filthy a few hours later.

The first thing we did was find the river. We all walked in, clothes and all. The water helped but we were still an unsightly looking group.

After we were somewhat dry, we walked up the river to some trees. There was a hobo camo in that area and it became our home for the next year.

My dad built us a shelter from scraps of wood, tar paper, canvas, carboard, anything he could find. It wasn't much but it was something to sleep in.

We all went to work immediately picking cotton. After a day picking cotton we didn't care where we slept we were so tired. Then we picked citrus and then strawberries. Sometimes we walked ten miles to work and back. If we were lucky we hitched a ride, but that wasn't too often.

My dad was good at saving money and after eighteen months of living on the river he had saved enough to buy a Model T Ford truck. He built a frame on its bed and covered it with canvas. That was our new home.

With a vehicle we were able to travel to find work, so we headed for the fruit orchards of Northern California. We went from orchard to orchard picking peaches and prunes and living in the back of our truck.

To this day I can still feel the peach fuzz on my skin itching and the peach bags cutting into my shoulders and hurting my back from the heavy weight.

I hated the work but I never complained. What good would it have done, I had to work and at least we wern't hungry anymore. In fact that winter when we went back to Bakersfield we rented a small house. "Things were improving" my dad told us.

On the third trip up north to pick fruit I didn't return to Bakersfield with my family. While shopping one afternoon I saw a sign in a local cafe for a waitress. I lied to the woman telling her I was eighteen instead of fourteen and went to work.

My folks were upset. But they knew how much I hated their way of life so they let me stay. I promised them I'd be good, and after all, I'd see them next summer.

I found a room in a rooming house that would let me stay until I received my first paycheck, which was $20.00. I was so excited.

I bought me my first new dress and shoes. I also bought undies, (I'd never had any undies) a hair ribbon, lip stick, nail polish, and bobby pins. I spent all afternoon fixing myself up. I curled my hair, painted my nails..... I felt so grown up and beautiful that I cried. In fact I stayed in my room and cried all night because I was so happy. I lived in a nice room, I had a good job and money to spend. Life couldn't be better.

But I missed my family. I would have given anything if they could have seen me then. As it was, they never did get to see the new me. They were killed in a car accident returning the next summer.

My landlady helped me through that trying time, she became a second mother to me, and then my mother-in-law.

Her son returned home the following year from a cc camp and we married the next summer on my seventeenth birthday July 6, 1939.

I survived the Great Depression but I pray to God our Nation never goes through a decade like that again.

CALIFORNIA COWBOY

Rusty B.

I was a cowboy in Oklahoma when the dust started blowin',
The cattle soon disappeared and ranchers were in despair and remorse.
It was 1933, there was great uncertainly across the state.
I was still a cowboy but there was no cattle and I had no horse.

So with my saddle and chaps I headed west,
I heard there was a big rodeo in San Francisco.
With a little luck I made a few bucks, then hitched a ride to Sacramento.

I found work in Loomis, a ranch just east of town.
I was a transplanted cowboy, I guess the hard times were to blame.
My fate had been sealed so I never looked back,
An Okie Californian Cowboy was what I became.

GLAMOR DURING THE DEPRESSION

Inez

Although the Nation was deep in a devastating depression glamor and beauty still existed and thrived during the 30's.

I was a high fashion model from 1933 to 1941, at which time I gave up my career to marry and raise a family.

I have wonderful memories of the thirties and some very prestigious honors. In 1934, I was one of the models that participated in the Chicago World's Fair. It was during that time I had the privlege to model the first bra to go on sale to the public. Most young women today don't realize how recent the bra is in our society. And even though it made its debut during the depression when money was scarce, it was a big hit, and of course, all of us women know why.

I also modeled the ladies Fedora hat, which didn't really catch on in fashion until the late thirties and early forties.

In a shear satin clinging gown, I modeled for a Kotex ad "no tell tail lines" the first beltless pad.

During that time I worked for Listerine. I was one of the "always a "bridesmaid, never a bride" girls, unless, of course, you used Listerine.

The most harilious modeling job I had was for a rubber bathing suit (made by one of the big rubber companies but I don't remember which one.) My body was powered and then it took three people to yank and pull the one piece suit up into place. It didn't look too bad but I was miserable in it. When the suit was removed after the showing my body was blistered every place it had touched me. Needless to say, the bathing suit was not a big success.

Over all, the thirties were very good to me. I lived in the world of high fashion and glamor and loved every minute of it.

I wouldn't trade those memories for anything. I guess I was one of the lucky ones.

DEVIL STORM

Martha

My husband and I were caught in a Devil Storm (that's what our Pastor called the black dust storms) one Sunday afternoon on our way home.

First the wind started blowing, then we could see the thing coming as if trying to catch us from behind. The whole country side was black behind us.

My husband drove as fast as our old vehicle would go, but still, we lost the race, it caught us.

We drove with our headlights on and our jackets over our mouths so we could breathe. By the time we got home and put the car in the barn we could see where pebbles had chipped the paint. That was our worst dust storm.

A FAMILY'S SURVIVAL

Sharon

I was born in the dust bowl. Of course it wasn't the dust bowl then. The dust storms started blowing when I was about 10 years old. A few years before that the drought started.

My parents had a small farm in the Oklahoma Panhandle and they depended on rain for their crops. So when the rain stopped, the land turned to dust.

For awhile we managed to grow a few vegetables and my father sold them to local grocery stores. Before long there wasn't even enough water to grow weeds.

I can still remember my father's famous words. "The drought will be over soon, it can't last forever."

But we weren't even skimping by and at night I could hear my mother "We can't stay here. We are slowly starving," she'd cry. And of Course my father's words would follow, "the drought will be over soon, it can't last forever."

My mother was a good housekeeper but when the wind blew there was dust on everything. We couldn't keep it out of the house. On the most severe storms we'd cover the windows with sheets and mom would make a tent with bed covers over her bed and make us kids get under it with damp rags to hold over our faces. My sisters and I were always scared and our brother called us babies.

One day our brother was caught out in one of the biggest storms to hit our area. By the time he got home he was sick. I'll never forget how he coughed and coughed, spitting up bloody dust. Nothing my folks did could save him. He died two days later on his 13th birthday. That was the worst day of our lives.

My dad loved his farm but after my brother died he said we had to move, he wasn't going to bury another child on his land.

We were packing to go to California, that's where most of our neighbors had gone, when my dad was offered a job on a cattle ranch in Colorado where his cousin was working.

We spent the next three years on that ranch. A little house came with the job so the first thing we did was start raising vegetables again and selling them to the stores. That money was saved for our return home. And that happened in 1938.

By then the drought and dust stormes had started to ease up. Our old house was still standing but it took us a week to shovel the dirt and sand out. Despite the dirt, it was in good condition considering it long neglect.

My father was happy he hadn't lost his land like so many of our neighbors during that terrible time. His, and my mother's only heartbreak was losing their son.
Otherwise, we survived.

THE CHESS SET

Bill

During the thirties checkers was the favorite game board in my community. Everybody played checkers, old, young, men women and kids. By the time I was ten I had mastered the game and wanted desperately to learn to play chess. Unfortunately, no one in the area knew how to play, and that included the teacher in our one room schoolhouse.

So you can imagine my excitement when my mother's brother came to stay with us the summer I was thirteen and he told me he knew how to play and would teach me.

He said we could use the checker board but we would have to make the pieces ourselves. Every evening for two weeks we sat on the front porch cutting, molding and pasting of cardboard into castles, kings, queens, knights, etc.....
After we made the pieces we tediously painted each one.

I'm sure it was a funny looking chess set but I didn't know it. To me it was the best looking game in the world. While we made the pieces my Uncle taught me the rules so the only thing I needed by the time we finished was hands on experience.

I'll never forget that first game. As my mother watched I saw a tear fall from her eye. She said it was happiness. I guess it was. She was happy I had accomplished a dream.

Those chess games are some of my fondest memories, and I might add, I became quite an accomplished chess player. My only regret is I never saved that home made chess set. What I wouldn't give to show it to my grandkids today to let them know, where there is a will there is a way. All you have to be is determined.

More people left the United States in the 30s than entered it.

There were more suicides during the depression than any other decade.

The thirties gave birth to such slang words as "Okie" and "Fruit Tramp." Okie, because more people left Oklahoma than any other state to come to California, and they came to pick the fruit.

AN OKIE FAMILY

Peter

I was second in a family of seven kids. The stock market crash of 1929 didn't affect us. We didn't even know what the stock market was. We were poor dirt farmers in Oklahoma before the drought and depression and starving poor dirt farmers by the mid1930's.

The dust and drought was our enemy. We didn't have enough water to even grow weeds. And the wind blew. Oh Lord, how it blew. It blew until you thought you'd go crazy. We had to hold rags over our faces when we went outside so we could breathe. A lot of people wore goggles, we didn't have any, so our eyes always stung and felt grainy.

I was twelve when my father decided to call it quites, like so many of our neighbors, and move to California.

Our old car, I think it was a Ford, was packed so tight we couldn't move. My folks and the 3 youngest rode in the front. The rest of us was in the back among our few possessions.

In order to save what little money we had for gas, we hunted jack rabbits, squirrels, and even fished when we could, for our evening meals, which was our only meal of the day. We were always hungry and the baby and my two year old sister cried all the time. I think my mother cried a lot too, just not in front of us kids.

Once, in the middle of the the Arizona desert we ran out of gas. We put the youngest three kids in the front seat, the rest had to walk. My dad tied a rope to the front bumper and he, and us older kids pulled that son-of-a-b......en car about 15 miles. I know it was at least that far because it took us two days to do it.

When the gas station owner saw us he knew we were in trouble. He put cream on our blistered hands and gave us a loaf of bread for supper. He even brought my mother a glass of goats milk. He stood by until she drank every bit of it. I think he was afraid if he left she'd give it to the babies and he knew she needed it.

We arrived in Bakersfield with 75 cents and a half a bag of dried beans. Beans were bought in big bags back then so there was enough to feed us for a couple of days.

Dad found us a job the next day picking... I think it was oranges and we moved into a farm labor camp. The camp boss called it a cabin but it wasn't anything but a wood frame with a tent top. You had to leave the door open for air and light.

Five of us kids went with dad that first day to pick. I remember we only made about $1.00, but we had never picked before. By the end of the week we were making about $3.00 a day.

I'll never forget that first payday, dad bought all us kids a candy bar. I can't recall anything since tasting as good as that candy did.

Most people in the camp was like us, from the dust bowl area and we soon learned the local people called us Okies and fruit tramps. We didn't care, as long as they let us work.

The second year we were in California my older sister married into another Okie family. My dad said he was sorry to lose a good worker, but my mother cried. I think she wanted a better life for her daughter.

Those were hard times but pulling together we survived and eventually was able to buy a small farm in the Bakersfield area, so in the end, this Okie family did get a better life.

BIRTHDAY NAME HUMOR

I came into the world during one of Oklahoma's worst dust storms. The dust and sand blue for three days and nights.

My father, being a little bit of a joker, gave me the name of Sandy. Unfortunately for me, it wasn't until I started school that we found out a girl's name was spelled Sandi.

My folks lived in Kansas when I was born. My mother said I was the dirtiest baby she'd ever seen, she had to dust me twenty times a day. So what else could I be named but, Dusty.

I was born in Oklahoma in 1935 during a violent dust storm. My first cry rang out just as the cellar door blue off it's hinges. So what's my name? What else, Celardore.

What does Box Car Willie and I have in common? Our names, of course.

My teenage parents were hitching a ride in a box car June 14, 1937 from San Francisco to her parents house in San Diego. They thought they had time, but I fooled them. My dad said the railroad men were so surprised to find out a baby had been born in the box car that they paid for a cab to take us to my grandparent's house.

The stock market crash wasn't the only news October 29,1929. I was also born that evening.

My father, who was a clerk on Wall Street lost his job two days later. To remember his first job loss and the irony of the event, he named me Crash.

Scooter King
OUR FINEST ROLLER BEARING SCOOTER
YOU CAN BUY ONE FOR YOUR BOY AT A
Good Saving
$3.98
What fun a boy can have with a Scooter—and what good out-of-doors exercise it is also. This is our finest Scooter and it is a very durable one. Has a specially designed roller brake, non-skid step, roller bearing wheels and a parking stand. The frame and front fork are of strong steel, and there is extra bracing beneath the platform. The footboard is made of natural color hardwood, varnished, and is 5½ by 13 in. in size. There is also a corrugated rubber step mat to prevent the foot from slipping. The double disc steel wheels are 10 in. in diameter and run on noiseless roller bearings. Oversize corrugated 1-in. cushion tires. Steel steering shaft. Hardwood handle bar. Finished in enamel baked on—the frame being bright red while the wheels are bright red with bright yellow stripes. The entire length is 38 in.; the height 34 in.
448 N 1862—(Ship. wt., about 15 lbs.) Each. . .$3.98
It is easily put together
PARKING STAND
ROLLER FOOT BRAKE

SKATE BOARDS

Barny

A young group of boys with baggy pants and caps turned backwards whizzing down the side walks on skate boards.
Sound familiar?

Yeap, it's me and my friends straight out of the thirties. Well, there are a few differences between the skate boards of today and the scooter boards, as we called them when I was young.

For example, our wheels were taken off old skates and were nailed to pieces of wood. Because of this, our boards didn't have much flexibility. So to control the board we fastened a stick to the front. Then we'd jerk up on the stick lifting the front of the board so we could control and manoeuver it around people and corners. We couldn't do the tricks that today's boards do but boy could we fly.

And as for the baggy pants, we didn't wear them for fashion, we wore them because they were hand-me-downs and we had no choice. And our caps were not baseball hats but tams with small bills which had to be turned around backwards when riding our scooter boards. I think that was an unwritten scooter board law.

What puzzles me is, why didn't we think of the name, Skate Board.

CINDY"S QUILT

Julie

I was young, only eight years old when I made my first quilt. It was during the depression and no one had money for bedding. So we made our own.

I can remember sitting for hours cutting out blocks from old dresses, shirts, jeans. We saved every piece of material we could use.

How proud I was when I made my first quilt. I loved it. I loved making quilts so much I never gave it up even when I finally out grew the depression and had the money to buy bedding.

When my girls were old enough we worked on quilts together. Both of them had made several by the time they were grown. So you can imagine my surprise when a few years ago I went shopping with my daughter and we wound up looking at new fancy ones. "Cindy needs a new quilt." She told me. Cindy was my thirteen year old grand daughter. I looked at the price and told my daughter, "you've got to be kidding. After all I've taught you, you wnat to buy a quilt, and at these prices." I was shocked.

She told me no body made quilts anymore and besides, today's teenagers don't want any "home made" stuff.

I couldn't believe my ears. after a lot of protesting, and because I think she was embarrassed, my daughter agreed to wait until I talked to Cindy before she bought the quilt.

Later that week, Cindy was visiting and I told her I wanted to made her a special quilt. a friendship quilt. One like I had made when I was a little girl during the depression.

I told her I wanted to use pieces of material from her favorite clothing, things she had outgrown but loved. Plus some pieces from her favorite teachers and special friends, ect...., anything that would make the quilt a remembrance. A quilt she would treasure forever. Her reaction was, "Cool"

Then I told her there was one problem. My hands were stiff from arthritis so she would have to help me. I never got a peep of protest. In fact, she was excited.

So we started collecting, cutting and ironing pieces. We'd only been working a few days when Cindy's best friend Jennifer asked if she could help. Before the week was over I had all eight of her friends over helping.

As they worked, the girls laughed, joked and gossiped. They told me about today's fads, played me the newest music and even showed me the latest dances.

At the end of every sewing day I'd get out my good china and we'd have an old fashion tea party. The girls enjoyed themselves and I hadn't had so much fun in years.

The highlight of the project came when we were almost through and Jennifer asked if we could make her a special friendship quilt.

Well, we wound up making nine quilts that year. I even showed the girls how to embroidery so they could all write their names on the quilts.

Of course I had to rub it in to my daughter. Teenagers don't like "home made stuff", hogwash. I think many of today's teenagers would like home made stuff if we took the time to show them like our mother's did when we were young.

I may have been young during the depression but I learned how to survive without buying everything.

THE NICKEL

By chance I found a nickel,
The year was 1935,
With it I bought some bread
And was able to stay alive.

By chance I found a nickel,
The year was 1998,
I let it lay on the street,
For what could I buy at its
Deflated rate?

THE HOBO

James

I was young, good looking, cocky, and impressed with myself in the 20s. I thought I knew everything and the world owed it all to me. So I headed for Chicago to give the town a gift of my knowledge.

With my attitude I was a prime target for the mobs that were running wild at the time, and before I knew what was happening I was in deep with one of the most famous.

I won't go into details but I crossed him and suddenly there was a contract on my life. I had to disappear, or I would disappear and I mean permanently.

The depression had hit the country by then so I felt I could lose myself in the homeless men wandering the states looking for work. I changed my first name and hit the rails.

The hobo life wasn't too bad. The worst part was watching the families living the same way. It was bad enough for a man, but for the women and children......

I tried to help as many of these desperate people as I could. I gave them what food I could spare and watched their kids while the parents searched for, or begged for anything they could use to keep their family together.

One time a man ran off and left his wife stranded in our camp with two small babies. The woman was so upset I feared she might throw herself and the babies into the river. I talked her into letting me take her to the relief center in town for help. I couldn't take care of her and she needed help desperately. The center said they could help, but I've never forgot the frightened look in her eyes as I left her there.

Two things I never did, was stand in soup line, and stay in a 10¢ flea ridden flop house. I had my own bed roll, which I washed often. Two shirts, an extra pair of pants, socks, and underwear, which I kept in my roll at all times. I even slept with my clothes under my blankets, it helped to keep everything pressed as all clothes had to be ironed back then.

Most hobos were always eager to share their tin coffee (that's coffed boiled in a tin can) for information of where you'd been and if there was any work.

Jobs weren't easy to come by but I did manage to find a few, especially on the docks. I liked the work but I didn't dare stay too long. Unions were being formed at that time so of course, there always seemed to be trouble. I couldn't afford to be mixed up in any of that so I'd just take off. Sometimes even leaving my paychecks.

I was pouring concerete on Hoover Dam when my boss fell and broke both legs. I was asked to take his place. I felt safe enough to stay for awhile so I took the job. After about eighteen months I began to feel edgy so I moved on.

By the late 30s I was in Sacramento California working the docks when I met a special woman.

For the first time in my life I wanted to settle down. I felt enough time had passed since my Chicago days and besides most of the mobsters I knew were either dead or in jail.

We got married and moved to Oroville California. I never told my wife or daughters about my past until the late seventies. By then I had a strong urge to return to my home town and see if I had any family left alive. I did, and what a reunion we had.

If I could live my life over, I'd stay out of Chicago. I gave up my family and most of my youth and in the end gained nothing.

My advice to the young people of today is, don't be so impressed with yourself. And don't get mixed up with the wrong people. It will only hurt you in the long run. I know, I've been there.

DETERMINED TO BE A GIRL

I. L. C.

Being a poor teenager during the 1930's depression was nothing like being poor today. Even the poorest of girls now have several changes of clothing and shoes plus cosmetics for school.

Me, I had one good dress for school and church which was removed immediately after arriving home. I washed my dress twice a week by hand. I refused to let my mother put it in with the regular wash as she used lye water and a wash board and I was afraid the material would fade.

It was important for me to look as nice as I could. Every night I rolled my hair in rags so I could have curls the next day. I also pressed my dress and hair ribbon, which was nothing but a hemmed piece of material that matched. It was a lot of work but it kept me wrinkle free.

I didn't have money for cosmetics so I improvised my own. After all, no teenage girl wants to stink from perspiration. I picked mint leaves, put them in a jar of water and every morning I dipped a cloth in the water and wiped my underarms. I kept the cloth with me during the day and only had to rewet it for another dose if I felt I needed it.

For face cream and body lotion I used lard. Not much, just a smiggen on each cheek, arms or legs. Then I wiped the excess off with mint water. That kept my skin smooth plus I always smelled good.

I"ve never forgotten the year I was fifteen and needed new shoes and there was no money. My mother told me I'd have to wear my brother's outgrown boots. I cried all night.

After the crying was over I made up my mind to do my best about the situation. I had no choice. So I got up early and washed the boots good. Then I rubbed ashes in the leather to hide the scuff marks. After that I cut strips of material from an old dress of my mine and made new shoe laces with huge bows. Next I used my dad's sack needle and sewed matching material around the top of the boot. This made it look like I was wearing socks even though I had never owned a pair.

When I showed up at school the next day my friends were impressed with my new shoes. I must admit they didn't look too bad, and best of all, I still looked like a girl.

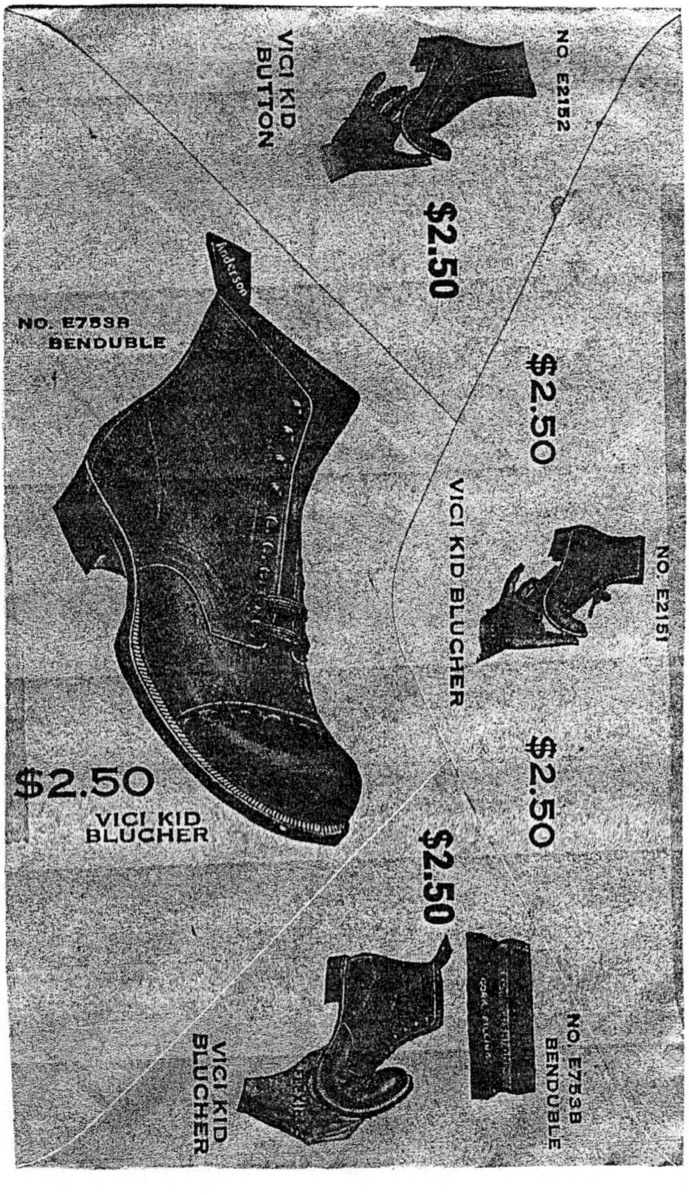
NO. E2152
VICI KID BUTTON
$2.50
NO. E753B BENDUBLE
$2.50
VICI KID BLUCHER
NO. E2151
$2.50
$2.50
VICI KID BLUCHER
$2.50
NO. E753B BENDUBLE
VICI KID BLUCHER

SETTLED FRUIT TRAMPS

No Name

I was born in 1921 so I remember the depression quite well. My family was poor, we were what you might call, "settled fruit tramps" by that i mean we picked the fruit but never followed it.

My folks had a shanty, it couldn't be called a house by today's standards, out behind Palermo California. There wasn't much out that way back then, just a lot of space and weeds.

I had three brothers and one sister, and we all worked. We started picking the early peaches in Red Bluff, then moved to the peach and prune orchards in Gridley.

Next came the olives. We picked Olives until the first freeze. After the freeze we knocked the trees and picked the olives off the ground, these were made into olive oil.

Back then we grew all our vegetables so we had a huge garden and my mother canned fruit and vegetables for the winter.

We never had any extra money but we never went hungry and we always had clothes to wear.

For entertainment, and for food, we fished and hunted. We also did a lot of swimming in the Feather River. But my favorite pass time was hunting rattle snakes. By the time I was grown I had a sack full of their rattles,

I attended the old wood two story school house in Palermo. I started High School in Oroville but never finished. When I was fifteen I lied about my age and went to work with my older brother in a logging camp. My brother was killed the following year, 1937 in a logging accident.

I stayed in the logging business all my life, except for the three years I spent in the Army.

Over All, I think I had a good life. I was raised to respect others and to work hard. I was also taught nobody owes you a thing, you have to work for what you get.

People try to tell me times have changed and everone deserves a piece of the pie. I say poppycock. Those of us that lived through the great depression, and worked to overcome it and survive know, people cannot take pride in therselves enless they work, no matter how hard the work is.

CALIFORNIA FRUIT TRAMP

From the dust bowl parires they came,
their dream was only to survive,
Milk for their babies,
bread for their children,
that was the beginning of the California Fruit Tramp.

Mattresses tied to their vehicle's top,
water bags hanging from the front,
a kit to fix their flat tires,
willing to travel and eager to work,
they headed for the next farm labor camp,
that was the life of the California Fruit Tramp.

Where are these people today?
they've disappeared from our orchards and fields,
a forgotten people lost to history,
along with all the farm labor camps,
a fleeting memory of long ago,
gone are the California Fruit Tramps.

ELKO

THE GARDENS

Ruth

I grew up on an arkansas farm. When the depression hit our area my father was still able to farm his land.

We mostly grew vegetables, but because of the low prices he was getting, he had to let his help go. Us kids became his farm hands.

During the harvests, he'd hire a few local town boys to help out, but that was it. The rest of the time we did all the farm labor.

My dad didn't like for anyone to go hungry. He had a small field that grew wild greens. He let anyone from our area pick all the greens they needed to eat.

He also had three acres close to town. He set this aside for the town folks to grow their own gardens. For some, the garden and their chickens, (everyone had chickens back then no matter how small your yard was) was their only food sorce.

Everyone tended their own garden. You'd see parents, kids, even grand parents working together growing their own vegetables. And there was no theft, everybody respected each other's plot of ground.

I doubt that kind of togetherness exists in neighborhoods today, or for that matter, in families.

DEPRESSED LIFE

No Name

I was born in the Northern Mid-West. I came from a poor family and married too young into another poor family. I started out poor and stayed poor all my life.

I married in 1931 and had no idea the Nation was in the middle of a devastating depression. I never heard any news and never went into town very often. When I did, my husband never let me talk to anyone.

I did hear a few people talking about some people being homeless and hungry. But I was hungry myself so I didn't understand what they were talking about.

We lived on a ranch and my husband worked when he was sober. The rancher furnished us a cabin. Actually, it was a shack, and a miserable one at that.

My first shack was one small room with a wood stove for cooking and heating. we had a straw mattress in one corner and some wooden boxes for our few possessions.

There was a make-shift table beside the stove for preparing food and washing. a shelf above it held my two plates and one cast iron skillet.

I was kept busy with cutting wood and raising a garden. There was fruit trees on the ranch so I was able to pick all we could eat.

I hated the winters because all I did was huddle by the stove and listen to the wind blow outside. The shack was always cold, I couldn't keep it warm.

The next spring a family that moved out of the area gave us a table with two chairs. I could finally sit down to eat.

My first baby was also born about that time on the old straw mattress with the help of a mid-wife.

By then I had a few chickens and sold eggs for a little money. I bought five yards of flannel for 50 cents and made my baby clothes.

We moved to another ranch and another shack by the time my second baby was born. It was closer to town so I walked to the Salvation Army and they gave me some clothes for me and my babies.

By then I had learned to hide what little money I made otherwise my husband would take it from me and go get drunk.

Life wasn't easy. I missed the depression all together, but then I was depressed myself.

It became easier for me in the forties when we moved to California to work in the fruit. Because of our big family we were able to make enough money so we didn't go hungry anymore.

In those days it wasn't easy for a woman to leave an abusive husband like it is today. Today, no woman has to put up with such a depressed life.

THE DUST DIDN"T BEAT US

Jackson

My folks owned five acres in western Oklahoma when the depression began. My dad worked for a local diary farm. On our land we had a small apple orchard and a very large family garden. Our extra fruit and vegetables we sold to town folks.

Things weren't too bad until the dust storms started. Until you've seen one you can't imagine what it like. All you see is a huge black cloud rolling towards you for miles and miles, and there is nothing you can do to stop it.

If the storm overtook you before you could get out of its way , you couldn't breathe. Several of our neighbors died from dust pneumonia (as it was called).

In 1935 my dad lost his job. The local diary, fearing for his cows, shipped them to his Uncle's diary in eastern Oklahoma. That part of the state wasn't hit by the dust storms like we were.

I was 14 at the time and every bit as large as my dad. In fact he considered me a young man. So he and I took off for Oklahoma City in our old car looking for work.

I found a job first. It was in a bakery helping an old couple. Their daughter had just married and moved to Texas.

I worked six days a week from 3am to 5pm for $1.50 a day and all the day old bread, rolls and pastry I wanted.

My dad got a job a couple of weeks later driving a delivery truck for a grocery store. Between the two of us, we made about $3.75 a day plus all the baked goods we could eat. We rented a house for $15.00 a month and sent for my mother and two younger brothers.

We lived in Oklahoma City about 3 years before my folks went back home. I stayed and continued working for the bakery another couple of years and then joined the army. I was in the military until I retired in 1968.

I can't complain about my life. It wasn't too bad even during the depression, or for that matter, the war.

My folks reclaimed their land and lived on it until they died. Now one of my Nephews lives in the old house, and I might add, it never looked better.

CAMP PREACHER

John

My most memorable memory of the depression was the night I heard my father cry. My father was Pastor of our small Community Church and over a three year span he had stood by helpless as family after family, gave up and left our drought ridden area.

Most of his congregation packed up and headed for California where they thought they'd have a better chance of supporting their families working in the fruit orchards.

The night My father cried, was the night he locked his church door forever. I felt so bad listening to him from behind my curtain bedroom.

"We have to leave her, Ethel." He told my mother. "I have to follow my flock. We've got to go to California. Those people need me and I fear I've waited too long."

So we packed up all our belongings and left. My father chose Fresno California to settle in. With in a couple of week of arriving, we had a small house and my mother got a job as a relief teacher at the High School, while my father sat about learning of the location of the farm labor camps.

The second Sunday in California my father delivered his first sermon. My mother and I accompanied him that day. The camp wasn't very nice and the people looked awful ragged. But the look on my father's face that day was spiritual. He was where he belonged.

We didn't pass the collection plate. My father said he couldn't take any money from these people. But as we picked up the books after the service, we found pinnies on the boards the people were sitting on.

From then on, my father put a collection box in the back letting people give only if they wanted to. He said for some people, they felt they must give something for the Lord's work. It made them feel better no matter how small their contribution was. And what amazed me was, he always made his expenses.

My father had found his calling. For over five years he traveled the San Joaquin Valley preaching at the farm labor camps, or sometimes even in the fields, bringing the word of the Lord to the dust bowl survivers.

RELIEF

Julie

Before the depression my family lived a confortable life. My dad was a contractor and made good money. We had a nice house, a car (not everyone had a car back then) and enough money to buy what we needed but also what we wanted.

Then the depression came and it hit my father hard. There was no extra money so no one could afford to fix or remodel their houses. His jobs were few and far between.

Being a Morman and living in Utah, I also had a brother on a mission for the church at that time. So any extra money we had my folks sent to him so he could survive.

My father was painting the local school one summer when he fell off a twenty foot scaffle. He was hurt bad and only lived about six weeks.

We had no other family so we were on our own and terrified. My mother first sold the house, then the furniture and finally the car. Because people just didn't have the money she didn't get good prices and we soon exhausted all our finances. Also my mother never seemed to recover from my father's death so she was unable to work, that is, even if she could find a job.

So we had no choice we had to go on relief. Welfare was not like it is today. Back then it was called relief and you weren't given any money, only coupons.

Coupons for everything. And you had to stand in lines to get them. Because of my mother's health, I was the one who had to stand in those lines.

I remember once when I needed a pair of shoes I had to stand in line for over two houres to get the coupon. And when you're a fourteen year old girl that embarrassment makes a big impression on you. I never wanted to be on relief again.

I began studying hard. I took all the business classes I could and finally got a part time job at the City of Paris department store.

I graduated from high school at sixteen and immediately went to work for the local telephone company for $50.00 a month. I know that doesn't sound like much money. But back then it was enough to keep my family off relief.

THE PENNY PRESSER
Buck

I was born in 1933 in east Texas so I don't remember too much about the depression years.

I can remember hearing the grown-ups talk about the hard times the country was having. But in my home town everyone worked. My father, along with most of the other men worked in the oil fields.

Those that didn't work in the oil fields, worked in town or for the W.P.A. In fact I can recall my mother saying nobody in our town went hungry or was on welfare.

One of my fondest memories of childhood was when a friend of my father's came to visit us every few years.

The man had a penny machine and pressed pennies for a living. He worked fairs, festivals, or busy street corners of large cities.

You gave him a penny and for a nickel he would put the penny in the machine, crank the handle, and presto, a flat penny came out with the Lord's prayer printed on the back of the coin.

On one visit we must have had ten kids show up at the house with a penny and a nickel. I, myself, had three of these flattened coins. I wore them around my neck until I descovered girls. That was in the forties.

I hated losing my pennies but I did make three girls very happy

PRIDE IN WORK

Lucy

My family left Texas in 1937. My dad heard about people making money in California picking fruit. He'd been out of work for about 2 months and didn't want to wait until we were flat broke like many who had left our area earlier.

So we loaded our few possessions in our model T ford, tied our mattresses on top and headed out.

We slept along side the road and it took us about ten days to get to California and check in at one of the farm labor camps.

The cabin they assigned us was small, about 12 by 20 one room. There was no windows. For light and Ventilation you had to let down large wooden flaps from the outside, with the flaps down and the door open, it wasn't too bad inside.

In the back corner, I guess you could call it the kitchen area, was a large sturdy table that had two shelves over it. On one end of the table was a two burner kerosene stove. I remember how my mother marveled over that small stove. She'd had a wood stove at home so she thought this was a wonderful invention.

There was no running water. We carried all our water from the faucet outside the door. The whole camp shared the toilet and showers. There was even a couple of wringer washing machines. My mother had never used a washing machine before so she thought she was living in luxery.

After buying groceries my dad purchased two canvas picking bags for him and my brother. They would use the bags and ladders to pick the peaches in the top of the trees while me and my mother used buckets and picked the bottoms.

In those days peaches were ringed. That was my job. I was given a large ring that resembled a bangle bracelet, in fact I wore it on my wrist. If the peaches fell through the ring we left them on the ground. We took plenty of those home to eat.

Picking peaches was hard dirty work. The peach fuzz made you itch constantly and the tempture was usually over 100 degrees. That combanation, along with the work really zapped your strength. We'd quit work about 2pm, go home and shower then rest under the large shade trees. It seemed every cabin had a tree.

After the peaches were picked we picked up prunes. I didn't like the prunes at all. I was always crawling around on the ground. There was no way you could stay out of the hot sun.

My dad knocked the prunes off the trees in our set, there were four trees to a set, with a rubber mallet, then we all crawled around and pick them up. The families that had the most kids made the most money in the prunes and since there were only four of us we didn't make as much as we did in the peaches.

After the prunes were over we headed south and wintered in Porterville and waited for the cotton season. Between all the harvests we managed to make a living even in the hard times.

My parents installed the pride of hard work in us early. No matter what kind of work you are doing, take pride in it and do it well.

I've worked hard all my life. I never took a dime I didn't deserve nor a nickel I didn't earn. I think that's what wrong with a lot of young people today. The pride of hard work has been bred out of them.

THE BIRTHDAY CAKE

Sally Jo

My mother was a wonderful person. Even during the depression when we were as poor as church mice she kept our spirits up and our dreams alive. She saw the humor in everything.

"If you don't laugh at life, you may never laugh." She would always tell us when there was no money for any extras.

And this brings me to my most memorable memory of the depression and my remarkable mother.

It was my tenth birthday September 17, 1937, and I wanted a birthday cake. Why it meant so much to have a cake on that birthday I don't know, all I remember is, I wanted one.

I prayed for a cake. For a big white fluffy cake topped with fruit. I never stopped talking about having a cake. I even asked God to send me one. I never shut up. I think I was driving everyone crazy. My mother must have talked to our Pastor about my obsession with the cake because he pulled me aside one day after Sunday School to talk to me. His lecture was on making impossible wishes. I remember telling him, he didn't have any faith.

On the day of my birthday I ran home from school as fast as I could, almost flying into the house. And sure enough, sitting on the kitchen table was a big, round, beautiful white fluffy cake with sliced apples on top.

I screamed and danced. I even cried. I knew without a doubt God had answered my prayers.

My mother said the cake was also our dinner. I thought that was a great idea as I helped her set the table. I was so excited.

As my dad and my sister, and I sat down, Mom started to slice the cake. Her eyes were on me and I couldn't help but see the laughter in them. Suddenly I was horrified.

My beautiful cake was nothing but mashed potatoes with sliced apples on it.

My mother laughed handing me my part, then my dad and sister started laughing. "This is the best cake I ever had." My dad teased as he took a big bite.

By then all eyes were on me. I had to give in. I laughed too. We laughed for years over that mashed potato cake.

"Well you didn't tell God what you wanted it made out of." My mother said with laughing tears in her eyes.

God Bless my mother and her sense of humor. No birthday cake had even been so dear to me as that mashed potato cake.

MAIDS

Agnes

My grandmother told me most all white working class families had maids during the 1920s.

When the stock market crashed and money was hard to come by, these woman started doing most of their own housework.

My grandmother was one such person. She said she begged her employer not to let her go, she had five young mouths to feed. And when you're uneducated and black, maid service is the only work you could do.

It seems the woman felt sorry for my grandmother and agreed to keep her on, but she cut her work days to three days a week and paid her 50¢ a day, instead of the 75¢ she had previously paid her, plus a loaf of bread.

My grandmother never said a word. She just kept working and skimped by the best way she could. "When you have hungry kids you'll do anything to let them eat" she always say when she finished telling me this story.

My grandmother survived and raised her five kids on that ridiculous salary. In my opinion, the woman was a saint.

THE LETTER

Katherine

This is a letter written to us by by father while he was in Washington picking apples during the depression.

Dear Family,

I have just finished eating my evening meal at the cookshack and have a few minutes before I go to town.
I am enclosing $10.00 for you to save. We only have a few more weeks of picking left and then I will be home. I will send you the rest of my paycheck before I leave.
I am going to hitch-hike home as I want to save the bus ticket money. I think with what I have earned picking this fall we will be able to make it through the winter. I figure it will take me about two days to get home.
I am looking forward to eating some of your good cooking, biscuits and gravy, the food hasn't been that great here this year.
I am sorry Katie has been so sick. Tell her to stay in bed and get well. Give both of my girls love and kisses for me and tell them I will be home soon.

Don't worry, we will make it through the winter. These hard times won't last forever.

Your loving husband
Jim

A JEWELED LIFE

Helen

I don't remember too much about the depression. I do remember at first we had a big house, several cars, and servants.

Then the stock market crashed and my father lost everything. I guess he couldn't stand the embarrassment of the situation so he committed suicide leaving my mother and me all alone.

I was five at the time. I do remember one day we had a lot of money and then my mother said we were broke. She said we had to accept our life and make the best of it.

She sold our house and we moved into a smaller one. To me the small house was nicer because I was more comfortable in it.

My mother never worked and we never went hungry. In fact, we, she and I, would have very elegant tea parties with the one nice set of china she was able to keep.

"We live a very jeweled life." She would tell me during these parties."

I never knew what she meant by those words, I thought she must mean we had a jeweled life because we were so happy.

I learned the truth when I was fifteen. It seems my mother had some very expensive jewelry hidden away that no one knew about.

Over the years she would take the jewels out of their settings and sell the stones to a jeweler in New York. She was able to live the jeweled life to quite an old age.

My mother was a remarkable woman for her day. Unlike my father, she was able to live a happy life despite her modest means. To bad my father didn't have some of her strength.

THE KINDNESS OF THE CHURCH

Opal

the thing I remember most about the depression is my dad walking out on me and my mother when I was nine years old and leaving us with no place to stay or nothing to eat. It was 1936.

My mother cried day and night for about three days before she came to her senses and realized how hungry we were. That afternoon we stood in a soup line for a small bowl of bean soup and a slice of bread. I didn't like standing in the long line and I didn't get enough to eat. My mother told me not to complain and to be grateful for the food.

Two days later, our landlord made us leave our apartment with one suitecase and the clothes on our backs. We went to what my mother called a "flop house" for the night. We caught lice and then had to go to a public health clintic for treatment. My mother cried again. She said she was so embarrassed.

After that, we didn't sleep in any more flop houses. Instead, we started spending our nights in the doorway of a big church.

A Priest found us one morning before we could leave. He took us to the Sister's quarters, fed us, cleaned us up, and gave my mother a housekeeping job for room and board.

The Sister's gave me my school lessons and taught my mother how to type on a typewriter. With in six months my mother had a job with a local lawyer. From then on we were able to take care of ourselves.

I hate to think what would have happened to us if that kind Priest hadn't found us and gave us the help we needed to survive.

HITCH-HIKING

Earl

In 1929, just before the stock market crash, I bought my first car. It was a 1924 Star and I gave an elderly couple $50.00 for it. The vehicle was like brand new, right down to the curtains on the side windows. I was really proud of that car.

Then the depression hit and times were rough, work and money just disappeared. I took any job I could get, I worked for the W.P.A., C.C.C., and the P.W.A., I made a little money but it just wasn't enough.

I finally left my home state of Oregon for California. I wound up in the Salinas Valley where I was hired by a lettuce packing shed. I considered myself real lucky because on any given day the yard was full of men just waiting for someone to lose their job so they could work. I like the work and the pay was great, 45¢ an hour, that was very good wages back then.

By the late 30s I remember buying a 1931 Ford Raodster. The car was five months old and I paid $500.00 for it. I purchased it on time and my payments were $27.00 a month. I can't remember what happened to that car, I think I lost it, but boy, did I like it.

Like I said, times were hard, and I didn't realize how rough my girlfriend and her family were having it until one night I treated us both to the movies and she got sick. She told me she hadn't eaten for almost three days. I bought her a hamburger but her stomach could only hold about half of it.

I went back to Salinas when the lettuce season started and sent my girlfriend a ticket. She came down and went to work as a housekeeper in a boarding house for her room and board. We got married at the end of the season with a hundred dollars in our pockets.

I heard about work in Arizona but we didn't have enough money to get there so we hitch-hiked again. When we arrived, and until a room opened up where we could stay together, we had to live in seperate rooming houses. Life wasn't easy but we never complained.

One winter we took a job house setting for a couple in Idaho. Things didn't work out as we planned and we wound up collecting pop bottles to buy food, which most of the times consisted of flour and water pancakes without butter or syrup.

When we left Idaho to return home it was still winter. We had enough money for one ticket but neither of us wanted to be seperated so we decided to hitch-hike again. We were so grateful when a bread truck picked us up so we could go in the stores with him to warm up. Heaters were not common back then in vehicles.

We had some rough times starting out back in the 30s. But what wonderful memories we made. In the forties, as the Nation began to heal and the hard times were disappearing, jobs and living conditions got better. We survived and over the years managed to raise five great kids. It was hard but it's been a wonderful life.

THE MIGRATION

Roy

From my family's Mojava desert service station on old route 66, I saw the Okie migration first hand. From the time I was a young boy until I was a teenager they passed through our area. Old mattresses, chairs, old pieces of furniture tied on top of their vehicles while pots and pan and water bags hung on the ourside.

Most Okies had Model T's and sometimes we could hear their wooden spokes rattling before we could even see them. I don't think too many young people today realize old Model T's had wooden spokes and when that dry desert air hit them the wood began to shrink causing the rim to rattle and clatter.

We had an old horse throgh back of the station that was kept full of water so the travelers could soak their rims, that usually took a couple of hours. So they rested, cooked and ate if they had any food.

Most Okie travelers were a pitiful sight back then. So my dad would let some of them stay for a few days, while they rested and rapaired or maybe washed a few clothes.

We didn't have much but I knew we weren't as poor as these people. I felt real sorry for some as they had nothing.

All the men seemed to think they were going to have a better life once they reached the fruit orchards of California.

My dad tried to help all of the Okies with food and repairs but some he couldn't. When I asked him why, he said. "Son we do what we can for these people but we can't help them all, there's just too many." And there was, they came......and came.... for years they came stopping for gas, repairs, and to soak their spokes.

I'll never forget one paticular family in trouble. Their car needed a gasket, they couldn't afford to buy one and my dad couldn't give him one, I know he wanted to but he had given them so much all ready.

Anyway, my dad helped the man take an old Prince Albert tobacco can and hammer it flat, then they cut it, and believe it or not, it worked. The family was off the next day.

Thinking of this story makes me wonder if maybe my father started the first R.V. Park? Of course the Okie's weren't on vacation but they were travelers and sleeping in their vehicles. Makes you wonder, doesn't it? What a difference a few decades makes.